# YOUR HUMAN DIGESTIVE SYSTEM
## OWNER'S MANUAL

## *FROM HEARTBURN TO HEMORRHOIDS*
### *(And Everything In Between!)*

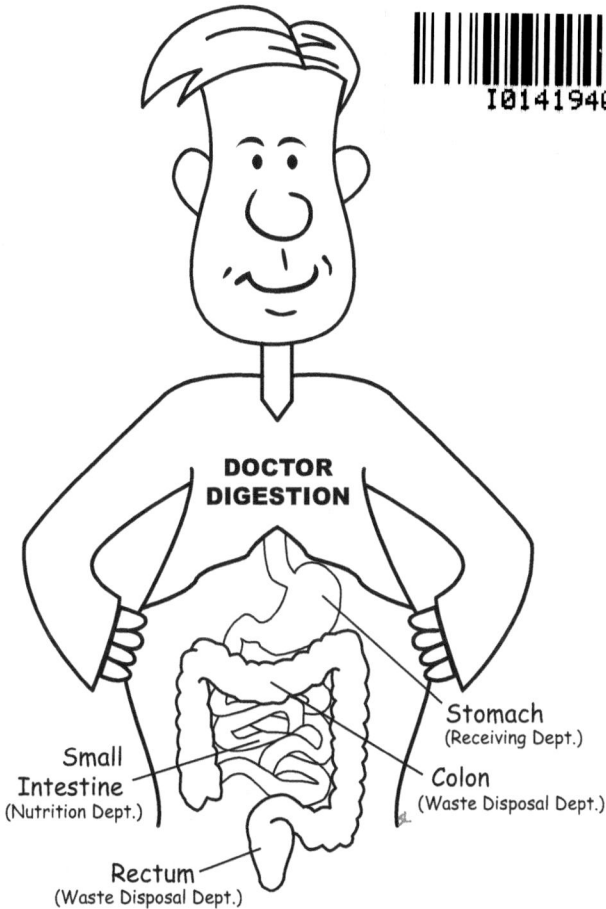

I0141940

DOCTOR
DIGESTION

Stomach
(Receiving Dept.)

Small
Intestine
(Nutrition Dept.)

Colon
(Waste Disposal Dept.)

Rectum
(Waste Disposal Dept.)

## James A. Surrell, M.D.
Fellow, American College of Surgeons
Fellow, American Society of Colon and Rectal Surgeons

# James A. Surrell, M.D.

Published by
**BEAN BOOKS, LLC,** Newberry, Michigan
sosdietdoc@gmail.com

Designed by Stacey Willey
Illustrations by Stephanie Lake

ISBN # 978-0-9825601-6-7

# Table of Contents

# Introduction To Your Personal Digestive Health

The following is a question that I truly believe we all should occasionally ask ourselves. "Who is ultimately responsible for my personal health?" Of course, the correct answer is, "I am the one who is ultimately responsible for my own personal health." Certainly, we all receive health care from our health care providers, and we also receive valuable additional health information from our health care providers, and also from other sources. These other health information sources may include family and friends, from reading, from the internet, and from various other media sources. Let me strongly suggest that we all need to carefully assess some of the digestive health recommendations found on the internet and elsewhere. I always recommend that you look to see if these health care suggestions are truly based on proven medical science, or are they based on, "What are they trying to sell me now?"

We also need to remain aware that our human digestive system represents a very major part of our internal organ system. Our digestive system contains the major components of our stomach, our small intestine, and our large intestine (colon and rectum). Of course, our mouth, our esophagus, our liver, and our pancreas are also essential parts of our digestive system. All of these components work together to allow us to maintain our personal health by taking in and processing our food and drink choices. All of these components of our human digestive system are reviewed for you in your following short and simple Human Digestive System Owner's Manual. I thank you for taking the time to learn all you need to know about our human digestive system, *From Heartburn to Hemorrhoids (And Everything In Between) – Your Human Digestive System Owner's Manual.*

# 1. Human Digestive System Anatomy
# Your Internal Food Processing Factory

We should all think of our digestive system as a food processing factory, with three departments that we all carry around in our belly, or abdomen. The first department is the stomach (receiving department). The second department is the small intestine (nutrition department). The third department is the large intestine that includes our colon and rectum (waste disposal department).

The process of digestion begins with the food or drink contacting the saliva in the mouth. Swallowing then occurs and the food or drink passes down the food tube (esophagus) to the stomach (receiving department). The esophagus is really a muscular tube that uses muscular contractions to push the food or drink from the mouth down into the stomach.

**Stomach** – Once the food or drink arrives in the stomach (receiving department) it is mixed with a potent acid called hydrochloric acid. Through muscular contractions the food is mixed in the stomach with this stomach acid, and the process of digestion is well on its way. Following a full meal the meal stays in the stomach from about 30 minutes to two hours, depending on the amount of fluid and type of food we have ingested. Once it is mixed with hydrochloric acid it becomes a thick liquid, which is slowly released into the beginning of the small intestine called the duodenum.

**Small Intestine** – Now that the food or drink we have ingested has left the stomach and entered the small intestine, the nutrition department really goes to work. This is where the "action" is, and truly where "digestion" takes place. This small intestine is referred to as "small" because it is a flexible small muscular tube that is only about one inch in diameter. However, it is not small with regard to its length.  If removed from the human body, the small intestine would be approximately 20 feet long, but when in your body it is in a constant state of partial muscular contraction, so it is about 10 feet long. This long length of your small intestine provides a very large surface area where all of our nutrients are absorbed. Nearly all of your needed nutrients are absorbed in the small intestine and the length of time it takes for the food and drink to pass through your small intestine ranges from about four to twelve hours.

**Large Intestine (Colon and Rectum)** – The colon now receives this liquid from the small intestine and immediately starts absorbing water, while moving this "waste" out of your body. The colon then passes this liquid waste material up the right side of your abdomen, across the top of your abdomen and down the left side of your abdomen to the rectum. The rectum is the lower 10 to 12 inches at the end of your large intestine, where stool is stored until a bowel movement occurs. In the process of this waste material passing from the beginning of the colon down to the rectum, substantial amounts of water and electrolytes (sodium and potassium) are actively absorbed in the colon. By the time this waste material reaches the lower left side of your abdomen and goes on down to the rectum in the pelvis, it is much more solid because much of the water has been absorbed out of the waste material. The waste material, or stool, passes through the large intestine in about 12 to 24 hours.

It should be noted that the only absolutely essential department of our three department food processing factory is the small intestine, or nutrition department. Humans can live without a stomach, and without a colon and/or rectum. However, the human needs to have at least one-third to one-half of the length of its small intestine to absorb nutrients from the food and drink we consume.

In summary, think of the digestive system as your internal food processing factory with a receiving department (stomach), nutrition department (small intestine), and waste disposal department (colon and rectum). Most of our nutritional needs are absorbed in the small intestine, except for water, sodium, and potassium, which are primarily absorbed in the colon.

## 2. Heartburn and GERD
## (Gastro-Esophageal Reflux Disease)

In my medical practice, patients often tell me about their heartburn symptoms. Heartburn is very appropriately named. The personal symptoms of heartburn are a true "burning" painful sensation in the middle of the chest, usually located behind your breastbone, or sternum. It may occur anytime, but is also frequently experienced after one goes to bed, often with a full stomach from a late meal or snack an hour or two before bedtime. It may occur after one goes to sleep, but the severe burning pain will certainly wake you up! Then you head for the medicine cabinet looking for the chewable antacid tablets to try to get some relief. So what causes heartburn, and how do I deal with it?

The painful symptoms of heartburn come from the normal hydrochloric acid working on digestion in your stomach "refluxing", or traveling up into your lower esophagus. Now, the lining of your stomach is designed to resist the effects of this potent stomach acid, and it generally does so very well. However, when this stomach acid goes up and makes contact with the lining of the lower esophagus, it inflames the esophagus tissue and causes this burning sensation behind your breastbone. Unlike the stomach, the lining of your esophagus is not designed to resist the effects of this potent stomach acid.

You likely have heard the term GERD. GERD stands for Gastro-Esophageal Reflux Disease, and GERD is now a commonly used medical term to describing this "reflux" of stomach acid up into the lower esophagus. Normally, the stomach acid is kept down in the stomach by a small muscle at the junction of the lower esophagus and the stomach. However, this junction of the esophagus and the stomach may "open up" over time, and this allows the acid to contact the lower esophagus causing these painful GERD symptoms.

The diaphragm is a very large flat muscle that separates the chest from the abdomen. The esophagus passes through an opening in the diaphragm to connect with the stomach. If this opening enlarges, it is called a "hiatal hernia". Heartburn symptoms are very often seen with a "hiatal hernia". With a hiatal hernia, the opening in the diaphragm enlarges, and this allows the stomach to partially slide up into the lower chest and this allows for stomach acid reflux to occur, causing heartburn.

GERD symptoms should always be treated. It is important not only to relieve the significant heartburn pain from the acid reflux, but long-term acid reflux into the lower esophagus can also cause cancer at this site. Generally, there are three common ways to medically treat GERD. Heartburn symptoms may be treated by 1) antacid tablets or liquid, 2) over-the-counter medications, or 3) prescription medications. There are two general classes of these medications, known medically as Proton Pump Inhibitors (PPI) or Histamine 2 (H2) Blockers. Common brand names of PPI medications include Aciphex, Prilosec, Protonix, Nexium, and common brand names of H2 Blockers are Zantac, Tagamet, Pepcid, and others.

With GERD symptoms, it is **very important** to have a periodic upper endoscopy to directly look at the esophagus and stomach, not only to make a correct diagnosis, but to also check for any pre-cancerous changes. At this time, biopsies of the esophagus and stomach likely would be done, as determined at the time of the endoscopy procedure. Depending on findings, surgery may also be recommended to treat severe or advanced cases of GERD. Don't ignore these heartburn symptoms! See your health care provider, and take advantage of the many effective medications used to treat this very common painful medical condition.

## 3. Stomach and Duodenal Ulcers and Gastritis
## "My stomach hurts!"

Peptic Ulcer Disease – This is medically defined as an ulcer that has formed in the stomach or more commonly, in the duodenum. The duodenum is the very first part of the small intestine where our food and drink passes out of the lower part of the stomach into the small intestine. A peptic ulcer is defined as a sore on the lining of the stomach, the small intestine or the lower esophagus. A peptic ulcer in the stomach is called a gastric ulcer and a duodenal ulcer is an ulcer in the first part of the small intestine, just beyond where it leaves the stomach.

Know that our stomach makes very potent hydrochloric acid that acts on our food or drink to begin the process of digestion. The stomach contents then pass into the duodenum so the small intestine can absorb the nutrients we have taken in as our food and drink. It is generally agreed that nearly all stomach and duodenal ulcers are from our stomach cells producing excess stomach acid. This excess potent hydrochloric acid eventually causes inflammation and damage to the lining of the stomach and the duodenum, leading to the formation of these painful ulcers.

A dull or burning pain in the stomach is the most common symptom of a peptic ulcer. A person will generally feel the pain anywhere between their belly button and breastbone. The pain most often happens when our stomach is empty, often between meals or during the night. The ulcer pain may come and go and it will often go away when we eat something that absorbs the stomach acid or if we take antacids or acid reducing medications. A less common symptom from these ulcers is bleeding. If ulcer bleeding does occur, it may present as blood in the stool, as black tarry stools, or even as vomiting blood. Of course, ulcer pain and ulcer bleeding always needs to be promptly medically evaluated.

If a person has these common symptoms of peptic ulcer disease, it is very important to be evaluated by your health care provider, and an upper gastrointestinal (UGI) endoscopy will often be recommended to accurately confirm the diagnosis of ulcers. Even with very mild symptoms, a person may have an ulcer. Without treatment, stomach and duodenal ulcers tend to get worse. Much less commonly, ulcers may be caused by a bacterial infection in the stomach from Helicobacter Pylori. When this bacterial infection is properly diagnosed, it will be treated with appropriate antibiotics.

There are numerous very effective medications that are used to treat peptic ulcer disease, and many are now available without a prescription. There are multiple ways to treat peptic ulcer disease and the three most common treatments are as follows. Number 1 – antacid tablets (such as Tums) or liquid antacids. Number 2 – acid reducing Proton Pump Inhibitors (PPI) medications such as Prilosec, Protonix, Nexium, and others. Number 3 – acid reducing Histamine 2 (H2) Blockers such as Zantac, Tagamet, Pepcid, and others. My favorite ulcer treatment recommendation to reduce acid production and treat peptic ulcer disease is Zantac, 150 mg. taken twice a day. Generic Zantac is Ranitidine, 150 mg. and it is readily available without a prescription.

Gastritis – This is medically defined as inflammation in the lining of the stomach that is also believed to be caused by excess stomach acid causing this inflammation. There are no ulcers present with gastritis, but gastritis may well lead to the formation of ulcers if not treated with an acid reducing program. Of interest, if a person has gastritis, and they eat something, the stomach pain may get worse because of the food causing more acid production. This increased acid then leads to more irritation of the inflamed lining of the stomach.

The treatment of gastritis is generally the same as the treatment for peptic ulcer disease. Both conditions are considered to be caused by the excess stomach acid produced in the stomach. Gastritis symptoms are also generally very effectively treated with Zantac, 150 mg. once or twice a day. If you have any symptoms of Peptic Ulcer Disease or Gastritis, be sure to see your health care provider without delay.

# 4. Gallbladder Disease
## Upper Right-sided Belly Pain
## Symptoms and Treatment

Here are the typical symptoms of gallbladder disease. It almost always presents as having some pain in the upper right side of the belly (abdomen), just below the right lower ribs. This pain usually shows up right after eating some food, and may also make a person feel nauseated and sick with an upset stomach. So, let's discuss these symptoms and briefly review the following. What is the gallbladder, why does it give some people these symptoms, and how do you fix a gallbladder problem?

Let's look at gallbladder anatomy. It is a small oval shaped balloon-like structure, about 3 or 4 inches long and one inch wide, located just behind and attached to the liver in the upper right side of the abdomen. Its primary function is to store bile that is manufactured in the liver. The bile is then released into the bile duct (tube) system and empties into the upper part of the small intestine, in response to eating a meal containing fats. The function of bile is to help your digestive system absorb and digest these fats to be utilized for normal and necessary body functions.

These common gallbladder symptoms of upper right-sided belly pain, nausea and/or vomiting are usually from something blocking the outflow of bile from the gallbladder into the small intestine. This bile duct blockage is most commonly from small gallstones that form in the gallbladder itself. These gallstones may then cause a blockage and prevent the gallbladder from emptying the bile, causing these typical gallbladder symptoms. Also, be aware that you can have gallstones present in your gallbladder and never have any gallbladder symptoms at all. Much less commonly, a tumor may also cause blockage of this bile duct system.

With the typical gallbladder symptoms noted above, one should certainly see their health care provider for evaluation and treatment. Most commonly, an ultrasound examination of the gallbladder will be ordered to look at the anatomy. This painless test looks at the gallbladder and surrounding structures and is the most common way to diagnose gallstones and/or abnormal gallbladder anatomy. If a patient continues to have these symptoms, and has had a normal gallbladder ultrasound, then an additional radiology test called a HIDA scan may be ordered. This HIDA scan offers the advantage of checking the gallbladder function and can detect an abnormally functioning gallbladder even in the absence of any gallstones or obvious blockage of the bile duct system. If this HIDA scan is ordered, your health care provider will give you more detailed information on this additional examination.

OK, so you have the gallbladder tests done and you are having symptoms from either gallstones or from a malfunctioning gallbladder even with no gallstones. At this time, surgical removal of the gallbladder (cholecystectomy) will almost certainly be recommended. This surgery is nearly always done as a minimally invasive procedure with several very small laparoscopic incisions with a very short hospital stay, or often as an outpatient surgery. Once the gallbladder is surgically removed, the bile manufactured in the liver now goes directly into the bile duct system. The bile is then delivered into the small intestine to continue its normal function to assist with the digestion of foods containing fats.

In summary, know that gallbladder symptoms are very common, and there are effective ways to accurately diagnose the cause of these often disabling symptoms. The standard of care is surgical removal of the gallbladder and this offers very effective treatment to eliminate these symptoms.

# 5. Liver Anatomy and Functions

Our liver is a vital organ that performs many functions in our body. The liver is one of the largest organs in our body, and the average healthy human liver weighs about 3 pounds. It is located in the upper right side of our abdomen just under or lower right ribs. If one could look at the human liver from the outside, we would see a larger right side of the liver and a smaller left side. These two sides are anatomically called the right lobe and the left lobe of the liver. These two lobes are separated by a band of connective tissue that anchors the liver to the abdominal cavity. The gallbladder, where the bile manufactured in the liver is stored, is found on the underside of the liver.

Our liver performs many functions and it is a very important organ with regard to our digestive system.

When we eat or drink something, it goes into the stomach where it is mixed with hydrochloric acid and the process of digestion begins. This food and drink then goes into our small intestine where it is broken down further to be absorbed into our blood stream. This blood coming from our intestines now goes into our blood vessels attached to our intestines. This blood now flows into our large abdominal portal vein to promptly flow up to our liver.

This blood flowing to the liver in our portal vein is now carrying our nutrients, any medications we may be taking, and also possible toxic substances. Our liver will convert many of the nutrients we consume as food and drink in our diet into substances that our body can now use to maintain healthy nutrition. The liver will then store these substances, and then supplies them to our cells when they are needed. Equally important, our liver will also recognize toxic substances that we may take into our body, and it will then convert them into harmless substances, and then make sure they released from our body.

Be aware that our liver plays a major role in the process of digestion in our body. Our liver is truly an essential organ for the digestion of fats. Our liver produces and uses bile to break down fats and produce energy. Our bile may be temporarily stored in our gallbladder, and will ultimately be passed into our small intestine where it is used for the breakdown and absorption of our dietary fats. Recall that fats are necessary for our health and nutrition and there is only one bad fat, known as trans fat.

Our liver plays a very key role in the digestion of carbohydrates. Our liver helps to ensure that our blood glucose stays constant. For example, if our blood sugar levels increase, the liver removes sugar from blood in our portal vein and stores it in the form of glycogen. If someone's blood sugar levels are too low, the liver breaks down the stored glycogen and releases sugar into the blood. Our liver also stores vitamins and minerals and releases them into the blood when needed.

The liver also plays an important role in the digestion of proteins. Our liver breaks down our proteins into amino acids so that they can be used to produce energy, or to make carbohydrates or fats. A breakdown product from our protein digestion is ammonia, and ammonia is a toxic substance. Our liver then converts ammonia to urea. This urea is then safely passed out of our body in our urine.

Our liver is also very important with regard to blood clotting. With the help of vitamin K, our liver produces proteins that are essential to allow our blood to properly clot when needed to prevent excess bleeding. Our liver is also one of the organs that will break down and remove old or damaged blood cells.

As noted above, our liver is a very key part of our digestive health system that performs many functions to keep us healthy. The bottom line is that we need to take good care of our liver, and it will continue to take good care of us.

## 6. What is My Pancreas, and What Does it Do?

Our pancreas is located behind the stomach in the upper abdomen. It is the organ likely best known to most people because it produces the hormone insulin, used by the digestive system to absorb glucose (sugar) from the bloodstream. It also produces glucagon, and this hormone has the opposite effect to release glucose into the blood stream to provide energy to our cells. The third hormone made in the pancreas is somatostatin, and it is also produced in the brain and in other parts of the body. The job of somatostatin is to regulate the release of both insulin and glucagon. The pancreas is primarily our digestive organ that produces our **digestive enzymes** to help us digest our food and absorb nutrients.

**Diabetes** – The major chronic malfunction of the human pancreas is Type 2 diabetes. This occurs when the pancreas cannot make enough insulin to store the excess sugar in the diet. Recall that the average consumption of sugar in the USA is about 150 pounds per person per year, or 3 pounds per week, and this equals about 42 teaspoons every single day. There are about 28 million Type 2 diabetics in the USA today, and 86 million "pre-diabetics", who will become diagnosed with Type 2 diabetes if they continue their present high sugar dietary choices. Unfortunately, this represents fully one third of our USA population, and is directly related to the monumental intake of dietary refined sugar in our diet. Fortunately, with good patient compliance, Type 2 diabetes can generally be effectively managed with insulin or with oral diabetes medications.

**Pancreatitis** – Inflammation in the pancreas is called pancreatitis. The pancreas produces chemicals called enzymes, and usually these enzymes are only active after they reach the small intestine. If these enzymes somehow become active inside the pancreas, they start to digest the pancreas itself. This can cause swelling, bleeding, and damage to the pancreas. Pancreatitis symptoms include severe abdominal pain, nausea and vomiting, fever, and the person generally looks and feels quite ill. The cause is often not known, but some medications, certain other illnesses, previous surgeries, and personal habits make you more likely to develop this condition. Acute pancreatitis is most often caused by alcohol abuse (70% of cases in USA). It is usually diagnosed with blood test abnormalities and a C.T. scan to look at the pancreas. Pancreatitis can become chronic.

**Pancreatic Cancer** –This is often referred to as the "silent killer", with no early symptoms, and often diagnosed at an advanced stage. When symptoms occur, they usually include pain in the upper abdomen and back, nausea and vomiting, loss of appetite, and weight loss. Diagnosis is often made on C.T. scan. Localized pancreatic tumors may be treated with surgery and advanced cases are considered for chemotherapy. In the USA, there are about 43,000 new cases each year, and nearly 37,000 deaths every year. Pancreatic cancer has one of the highest fatality rates of all cancers, and is the fourth highest cancer killer among both men and women worldwide. The overall survival rate for all pancreatic cancer stages is 25% at one year and 6% at five years. For localized pancreatic cancer, the five year survival is 20%. Be aware of various factors that increase the risk of pancreatic cancer. These include family history, smoking, overweight and obesity, diabetes, and others. Know your family history, don't smoke, maintain a healthy weight, and do not ignore any upper abdominal medical symptoms.

# 7. Appendicitis
# Lower Right-sided Belly Pain
# Your Surgeon is Now Your New Best Friend!

We all know someone, or perhaps ourselves, who have been diagnosed with appendicitis, and then had surgery to have their appendix removed. It is important that we understand the usual symptoms of this common medical condition, because if one has a developing infection in their appendix (appendicitis), and does not seek medical care, it can progress to become life threatening. Let us now take a closer look at this important and potentially very serious surgical health problem.

First of all, recall that the four letters "itis" on the end of a medical word mean inflammation or infection. We are all born with an appendix and this is a small tubular structure that hangs down from the very beginning of the colon located in the lower right side of your belly. It has about a one half inch opening where it is attached to the beginning of the colon, is about two to three inches long, and is closed on the other end. As long as this opening into this small sock-like structure stays open, there is no problem and the intestinal fluids and normal bacteria flow in and out of the appendix all day long. However, if this opening gets blocked off, usually due to unknown reasons, the normal bacteria are now living a closed space and they continue to multiply and swelling and infection will occur. Now we have an infected appendix, or "appendicitis".

Just how common is this "appendicitis"? It is estimated that there are about 250,000 cases of appendicitis every year in the USA, and current studies show that it will occur in about 7% of the population. Appendicitis is rare under age 2 and most commonly is seen between ages 10 and 30. For unknown reasons, it is more common in males than in females.

Here are the typical symptoms of appendicitis. First, a person with appendicitis will feel a vague discomfort and mild pain around the belly button (navel) and the patient always develops a near complete loss of appetite. Usually there is mild nausea, but typically there is no vomiting early on with a developing appendicitis. As the inflammation and swelling of the appendix continues, the appendix pain now moves to the lower right side on the belly as this now-swollen appendix comes into contact with local surrounding structures. We now have a developing condition called localized peritonitis, or inflammation of the lining of the abdominal cavity. The pain is now constant and worsening, usually with a developing fever. Things are now starting to get serious. If this inflamed appendix is not surgically removed, the appendix will continue to swell and eventually burst. This is known as a ruptured appendix, and the infection will generally now rapidly spread throughout the abdomen. We now have a serious potentially life-threatening surgical emergency.

Recall that six letters "ectomy" on the end of a medical word mean "to remove". Therefore, the treatment of appendicitis is for the surgeon to perform an appendectomy to surgically remove the appendix. Of course, it is much more preferable to diagnose a developing appendicitis and surgically remove the appendix before it progresses to the point of becoming a ruptured appendix.

**Bottom line** – If a person initially feels a mild pain and discomfort around their belly button that slowly moves down into the lower right side of the belly, then seek medical help without delay. Further, the patient with appendicitis will also experience a complete loss of appetite. With this typical history, see your health care provider or closest emergency department without delay. These health care providers will then take measures to properly diagnose and recommend urgent surgical treatment for the appendicitis.

## 8. Diverticulosis & Diverticulitis
## Lower Left-sided Belly Pain
## Do Not Ignore This Pain!

What is Diverticulosis? Diverticulosis is a condition in which pouches (or small sacs) form on the wall of the large intestine or colon. The pouches are about ½ inch or less in size, and are found most often on the left side of the colon. Most people with diverticulosis do not have any symptoms at all and they may never know they have the condition. With diverticulosis, you do NOT have to avoid seeds, nuts, popcorn, peanuts, berries, or any specific foods at all. A high fiber diet is highly recommended.

What is Diverticulitis? The term "diverticulitis" refers to an infected or inflamed pouch. The term "itis" on the end of a medical word means inflammation or infection. People with diverticulitis usually feel left-sided abdominal pain. People with diverticulitis need to be treated with antibiotics, usually as an out-patient, but more serious cases may need hospitalization and I.V. antibiotics.

How are these disorders diagnosed? Most often diverticulosis causes no symptoms and is often discovered by an X-ray or colonoscopy examination done for an unrelated reason. The doctor may see the diverticula (pouches) through a flexible tube (colonoscope) during a colonoscopy procedure. Patients experiencing the symptoms of diverticulitis with left-sided abdominal pain should see their physician as soon as possible to determine what is causing the symptoms.

How common are these disorders? Diverticulosis is very common, especially in older adults. Studies show that about 10% of Americans over age 40 years have diverticulosis, and about 60% over age 60 years. However, only about 10 to 20% of patients with diverticulosis ever have any problems such as diverticulitis.

Are these disorders serious? For most people, diverticulosis is not a problem. Diverticulitis is a serious medical condition. An infected or inflamed pouch can lead to serious infection called an abscess, or a hole (perforation) in the bowel wall. People experiencing symptoms should always see their physician without delay for a proper diagnosis and treatment plan.

How are diverticulosis and diverticulitis treated? If you have diverticulosis with no symptoms, treatment is not required, but you should follow a high fiber diet. Fiber-rich foods such as whole grain cereals and breads, fruits and vegetables, and other high fiber foods reduce pressure in the colon and promote a healthy digestive tract with a normal bowel pattern. I strongly encourage all my patients with diverticulosis to take one heaping teaspoon of sugar free Metamucil in water once a day, every day. This has been proven to significantly reduce the risk of recurrent diverticulitis. Patients with diverticulitis should be treated with antibiotics and possibly dietary restrictions. Severe cases may require hospitalization and possible surgery. Your health care provider is available to discuss diverticulosis and diverticulitis with you in greater detail.

# 9. Constipation and Diarrhea
## What is a "Normal" Bowel Pattern?

What is a "normal" bowel pattern? This is a good question and one that we should ask ourselves. Let's discuss constipation and diarrhea, the terms used to define these all-too-common medical conditions. Here's the definition – a "normal" bowel pattern would generally considered to be anywhere from three bowel movements per day to three bowel movements per week. However, if you have a change in bowel habits, it is very important to see your health care provider, to determine the cause. Further, always be aware that any over-the-counter or prescription medications may cause either constipation or diarrhea in certain individuals.

Our digestive system is made up of the stomach where food and drink enters the system, the small intestine where nutrients are absorbed, and the colon and rectum through which the waste material passes. The colon is also the organ that absorbs liquids to replace our water every day. Simply stated, constipation is waste material moving too slowly through the colon and down to the rectum. Diarrhea is food and drink passing rapidly through the our digestive system with frequent bowel movements. Be aware that dietary fiber is essential to solving both constipation and diarrhea. Dietary fiber cannot be absorbed by the human digestive system and it merely acts as a "sponge" that readily absorbs fluids.

**CONSTIPATION** – This is most commonly caused by not drinking enough water, and not eating enough dietary fiber. If a person does not drink enough fluid, the colon absorbs as much fluid as it can out of the waste material that enters the colon. This is done to prevent dehydration. The waste material in the colon now becomes thickened, and moves more slowly through the colon. This results in hard stools that become difficult to pass out of the rectum. If this goes on long enough, the rectum and all or part of the colon may become filled with hard stool, and this is medically called a fecal impaction. Medications that most commonly cause constipation are the more potent prescription pain medications.

**DIARRHEA** – This is the opposite of constipation and represents an abnormally rapid passage of food and drink through the digestive system. Diarrhea may be caused by infection, inflammation, medications, or stressful life events. It is important to note whether or not a person is having diarrhea episodes at night, during their normal sleep time. If there is no diarrhea interrupting one's sleep, it is very unlikely that there is a bowel infection or bowel inflammation (such as colitis), as the cause of the diarrhea. In certain individuals, antibiotics and some of the acid-reducing medications cause diarrhea. Stress may also cause diarrhea, most commonly seen with Irritable Bowel Syndrome (IBS).

For both constipation and diarrhea, I recommend 25 to 30 grams of dietary fiber per day, every day. I believe the powdered fiber supplements taken in water work the best. Fiber acts like a "sponge" in your colon. With constipation, fiber absorbs and hangs on to fluid in the colon and also pulls water into the colon, making the stools pass more easily through the colon and out the rectum. With diarrhea, the fiber absorbs the excess fluid rapidly passing through the colon, makes the stools more formed, and this slows down the passage of stool. Once the specific cause of the constipation or diarrhea is accurately determined, specific recommendations can be made by your health care provider to get your bowel pattern back to normal. However, the absolute key to very effective treatment for both chronic constipation and diarrhea is your two best friends of your digestive system, FIBER and FLUIDS.

# 10. Fiber and Fluids
## Daily Fiber and Fluids are Your Friends

There are many health benefits that come from taking in enough dietary fiber and fluids every day. Here are two medical terms you need to know. ***Ingestion*** is the process of taking food or drink into our body. ***Digestion*** is what happens to the food or drink in the human digestive system after we have consumed our food or drink.

**FIBER** – Remember that dietary fiber is something you *ingest*, that the human body cannot *digest*. In our body, this dietary fiber acts like a sponge to absorb fluid. The fiber in our food or drink enters the stomach, passes through our small intestine, and enters the colon. If there is excess fluid in the colon (diarrhea), the dietary fiber absorbs the excess fluid in the colon and makes for more formed stools and stops the diarrhea. If there is not enough fluid in the colon (constipation), the dietary fiber absorbs and keeps more fluid in the colon, and this makes for more frequent, softer, and easier to pass bowel movements. Therefore, because of the way fiber absorbs fluid, it will correct both diarrhea and constipation. Our digestive system needs fiber to work properly and we should take in about 25 to 30 grams of dietary fiber every day.

Excellent sources of dietary fiber include whole grain and whole wheat breads, fresh vegetables and fruits, and high fiber cereals. Original Fiber One Brand Cereal is an excellent choice with 14 grams of dietary fiber and zero sugar in a single ½ cup serving. If you are not a cereal eater, try using this product as healthy croutons on your tossed salad.

**FLUIDS** – Our human body is about 60% water, and we need to replace this water and rehydrate ourselves every day. Every system in our body needs water to function properly. Water carries nutrients to all our cells, and provides the fluid necessary for the proper function of our lungs, muscles, eyes, ears, mouth, throat, digestive system, and all body tissues. A good guideline is that we are well hydrated if we feel the urge to urinate during the day about every 2 to 3 hours. Further, our built-in thirst mechanism is very reliable. Therefore, if we feel thirsty, we may be low on fluid and possibly dehydrated, and our body is telling us to drink more fluid. Here is my short and simple 60/60 rule – since our human body is about 60 percent water, we need to take in about 60 ounces of fluid per day to prevent getting dehydrated.

Unless you are on a fluid restriction from your health care provider, drink at least 60 ounces of fluid every day. Your fluids may be water, coffee, tea, low sugar juices, or other fluids. This can easily be done by having 12 ounces of water or other fluid with breakfast, lunch, and dinner, and 12 ounces of fluid mid-morning and mid afternoon. Also, by not drinking too much fluid in the evening, this will likely reduce the need for you to get up to urinate during your normal sleep time. Recall that our human body is about 60% water, and we need to replace this water and rehydrate ourselves every day. Again, let me remind you that if you are on a fluid restriction from your health care provider, be sure to consult with them regarding how much fluid you should have every day.

Remember, fiber and fluids are your healthful friends. We need about 25 to 30 grams of dietary fiber every day and about 60 ounces of fluid every day. Remember to drink water with meals and throughout the day. Once you make this "fiber and fluids" program part of your daily routine, you will enjoy the many health benefits of proper hydration, and will be strongly motivated to continue.

# 11. Colon and Rectal Cancer
# Know the Colon Cancer Screening Guidelines
# and Know Your Family Health History

According to the National Cancer Institute, there are approximately 140,000 new cases of colorectal cancer and nearly 50,000 colorectal cancer deaths every year. The lifetime risk of developing colorectal cancer in both men and women is about 1 in 20. In men, it is the third most common life-threatening cancer, behind prostate and lung cancers. In Hispanic men, colorectal cancer is more common than lung cancer. For all women, it is also the third most common, behind breast and lung cancers.

Colorectal cancer is the second leading cause of cancer death in the United States and is one of the most preventable of all human cancers. Colorectal cancer is appropriately called the "silent killer," since most patients usually have no early symptoms. In fact, the most common early symptom of colon cancer is nothing at all. Therefore, do not ever believe that if you are having no symptoms and feeling well, that you should not have colorectal cancer screening.

Of course, if any symptoms are present, such as rectal bleeding, change in bowel habits, unexplained weight loss, unexplained anemia, or other digestive symptoms, then prompt evaluation of the colon is clearly indicated. Please remember this most important fact - the most common early symptom of colon cancer is nothing at all. This is why it is so important to follow these screening guidelines for this common but preventable cancer. Further, know that the risk for both colon cancer and colon polyps is significantly increased with smoking. It is now estimated that a person who chooses to smoke will increase their risk of colon cancer by nearly 20 percent!

So where does colon cancer come from? Colorectal cancer nearly always develops from polyps, which are small growths on the inner lining of the colon. Removing these polyps substantially reduces the risk of colon cancer. It is now estimated that perhaps 30 to 40% of the adult population have polyps. Of course, because polyps have no early symptoms, the vast majority of these people are not aware they have polyps. Screening in the form of a colonoscopy is the standard of care and it is a very safe, effective, painless method of visually examining the entire colon and rectum while the patient is made sleepy with a light sedation. Polyps that are found during the colonoscopy examination are removed, and any other possible abnormal findings can also be checked at that time.

So, here's the good news. Colorectal cancer is curable if detected early. For screening, a colonoscopy is recommended for all persons over 50 years of age even if they have no symptoms. With a family history of colon cancer or polyps, colonoscopy should be done at age 40, or 10 years before the age of the diagnosis of colorectal cancer in that family member. If polyps are found, or with a family history of colorectal cancer or polyps, a personal history of inflammatory bowel disease (colitis), more frequent examinations are generally recommended. Be certain to discuss this very important colorectal cancer screening with your personal health care provider. Do yourself and your family a favor and get screened for colorectal cancer.

In summary, remember that a colonoscopy should be done at 50 years of age even if there are no symptoms at all, and at age 40 with a family history of colon cancer or polyps. If there are any symptoms, such as rectal bleeding, change in bowel habits, unexplained weight loss, or any digestive symptoms, prompt evaluation of the colon is certainly indicated. Ongoing colorectal cancer screening recommendations are based on personal and family history, and on the specific colonoscopy findings.

## 12. Irritable Bowel Syndrome (IBS)
## Belly Bloating, Cramping, Frequent Loose Stools

A common IBS patient statement is as follows: "I need to find a toilet and go have a bowel movement – right now!" This is known as "stool urgency."

What is Irritable Bowel Syndrome? Irritable Bowel Syndrome, or IBS, is a very common disorder of the digestive tract. It affects the colon, or large intestine, usually over a long period of time. An estimated 20% of the population, or about 60 million people in the USA, suffer from IBS. IBS is a syndrome and not a disease, and should not be confused with Ulcerative Colitis or Crohn's Disease. Through the years, it has been called by many names, such as "nervous" colon or "spastic" colon. The term "colitis" should never be used to define IBS.

What are the symptoms of IBS? The term "syndrome" refers to a set of symptoms that occur together. The symptoms of IBS may include abdominal pain, gas, bloating, a change in bowel habits, diarrhea, constipation, or constipation alternating with diarrhea. Rectal bleeding is never a symptom of IBS.

What causes IBS? It is believed that most of the symptoms of IBS occur when the muscles in the colon do not work properly. The role of the colon, or large intestine, is to act as the waste disposal system of the body and to absorb water from the liquid stool that enters it from the small intestine. The stool then passes to the rectum where it is stored until a bowel movement occurs. The process is controlled by nerves and the muscles of the wall of the colon. In people with IBS, the muscles of the colon contract abnormally. An abnormal contraction, or spasm, may speed up the passage of stool, resulting in diarrhea. At other times, the spasm may delay the passage of stool, resulting in constipation. The exact cause of IBS is unknown. However, symptoms are worsened by emotional stress and a low fiber diet.

How is IBS treated? Once a person has been properly diagnosed with IBS and not a more serious disease, treatment recommendations will be made. Adding fiber to your diet has clearly been shown to lessen, or even totally eliminate, the diarrhea, constipation, and cramping symptoms of IBS. Dietary fiber is something you ingest (eat) that you cannot digest. The fiber passes through the stomach, through the small intestine and into the colon (large intestine). The fiber then absorbs water and liquid in the colon. If you have diarrhea, the fiber will absorb the extra water and fluid and will make for less frequent and more formed bowel movements. If you have constipation, the fiber will retain water and fluid in the colon and increase your number of bowel movements. Fiber also decreases spasms and painful pressure in the colon.

If needed for frequent stools and diarrhea, anti-diarrhea medications such as Imodium may also be recommended. Again, the key to very effective treatment of IBS is to add dietary fiber to one's diet.

I often recommend Sugar-free Metamucil, one heaping teaspoon in water once a day, every day. My further advice – only take your Metamucil on the days you breathe!

Can IBS lead to more serious problems? IBS has not been shown to lead to any serious disease such as colitis or cancer. All patients with IBS should work closely with their physician to lessen their IBS symptoms. By establishing a close relationship with your health care provider Irritable Bowel Syndrome can be effectively managed. Always remember that rectal bleeding is never a symptom of IBS, and rectal bleeding always needs to be evaluated by your health care provider to determine the exact source of the rectal bleeding.

## 13. Inflammatory Bowel Disease (IBD)
## What is Crohn's Disease, Ulcerative Colitis,
## Proctitis, and Microscopic Colitis?

There are various forms of Inflammatory Bowel Disease, often referred to as IBD. These include Crohn's Disease, Ulcerative Colitis, Proctitis, and Microscopic Colitis. It is very important to understand that these all represent true disease processes. These medical inflammatory conditions are never to be confused with or compared to Irritable Bowel Syndrome (IBS), because IBS never causes true inflammation of the human digestive system.

Inflammatory Bowel Disease (IBD) includes various true diseases of the digestive system. You should also know that "itis" on the end of a medical word means inflammation or infection, so "colitis" means inflammation in the colon and "proctitis" means inflammation only in the rectum.

Chronic Ulcerative Colitis (CUC) is a disease that involves inflammation of the lining of all or part of the human colon and rectum. It is limited to the colon and rectum and does not spread elsewhere. When active, CUC gives the patient symptoms of very frequent loose stools, usually with bloody diarrhea. Most often, it can be very effectively treated with various medications to reduce the inflamed lining of the colon and rectum. If there is inflammation only in the rectum, it is called proctitis. A variation of CUC is known as microscopic colitis, with no apparent abnormalities seen on colonoscopy, but there is cellular inflammation when biopsies of the lining of the colon are assessed under the microscope. Microscopic symptoms may include frequent loose stools and some rectal bleeding but these symptoms may be not as severe as those experienced with CUC.

If CUC or microscopic colitis does not get better with medical treatment, surgery may be needed to remove the colon and rectum and this will essentially cure this disease. The surgery may involve multiple procedures to remove and then possibly reconstruct the digestive tract. Further, with long-term CUC there is an increased risk for the development of colorectal cancer and CUC patients must be monitored very closely with more frequent colonoscopy examinations. CUC was first recognized and described in England in 1859.

Crohn's Disease was first described by three doctors in New York in 1932. This disease also involves inflammation in the digestive system, but may occur anywhere from the mouth to the anus. Crohn's Disease is very different from CUC for two important reasons. Number 1 – it is not limited to the colon and rectum and can be diagnosed anywhere in the human digestive system. Number 2 – it involves the entire wall of the digestive tract and not just the lining. Crohn's Disease most commonly occurs at the end of the small intestine (ileum) just before it enters the colon, located in the lower right side of the abdomen. The second most common site for Crohn's Disease is in the anal area. Crohn's Disease may also be less commonly seen in the colon, rectum, stomach, or duodenum. Because of these many potential sites of Crohn's Disease, it is generally more difficult to diagnose than CUC, as Crohn's Disease may mimic appendicitis, hemorrhoids, ulcers, or other more common conditions.

The cause of these Inflammatory Bowel Diseases is not well understood, but it is thought to possibly be an autoimmune disease, but we have much more to learn about the causes of IBD. Both CUC and Crohn's Disease are treated with various medications to reduce the inflammation, to suppress the immune response, or both. With failure of medical management or complications from IBD, surgery may be needed to further treat these diseases. To learn more about IBD, I highly recommend the Crohn's and Colitis Foundation of America as the best source of information, and their website is www.ccfa.org.

## 14. Refined Sugar Consumption in the USA and the Impact on Our Overall Health

The average sugar intake in the USA today is 150 pounds of sugar per person per year, or about 3 pounds per week, or about 42 teaspoons of sugar each and every day! As a result, 2/3 of adults, and 1/3 of children in the USA are now considered to be overweight or obese.

**Impact of excess refined sugar on overall health:**

- Primary cause of Overweight and Obesity Epidemic in the USA (2/3 of adults and 1/3 of children)
- Primary cause of Pre-Diabetes and Type 2 Diabetes Epidemic (114 million people in the USA)
- Pre-diabetes and Type 2 Diabetes both lead to major increased risk for Dementia and Alzheimer's
- Excess refined sugar, not eating fats or cholesterol, is the primary dietary cause of High Cholesterol
- Major cause of High Blood Pressure, because eating sugar causes increased absorption of sodium
- Doubles risk of Heart Disease – Journal of the American Medical Association (JAMA), 2/3/2014
- Heavy sugar consumption leads to increased risk of depression – (Psychology Today, 9/2/2013)
- Major cause of Dental Cavities and Poor Oral Health
- Life Expectancy is Decreased by 7 Years with Obesity, and by 4 Years if Overweight

Low Sugar → Lose Body Fat → Lose Weight – Every one of the 40 trillion cells in our body needs glucose for energy. This is why our body stores all excess sugar as body fat. However, if we take in less refined sugar, our body now has to burn body fat to get glucose for energy for all our 40 trillion cells. On the short and simple *SOS (Stop Only Sugar) Diet*, our body now burns body fat to get glucose to provide fuel for all our 40 trillion cells. When you follow the SOS Diet, our body must BURN BODY FAT to get glucose for energy, and you easily lose at least 5 to 8 pounds a month, have more energy, and are so much healthier! On the SOS Diet, say goodbye to body fat and excess body weight!

Lower Cholesterol - A major side-effect of the insulin is that it tells your liver to manufacture more cholesterol. The bad sugar news is this: High sugar → High insulin → High cholesterol. On the short and simple *SOS Diet*, you now have this good news: Low sugar → Low insulin → Low cholesterol.

Read labels for Low Sugar - Make the short and simple **_SOS (Stop Only Sugar) Diet_** a simple lifestyle change for you. When you become a "Label Reading Detective" and get all that refined sugar out of your diet, you will lose between 5 and 8 pounds per month, and you will be so very much healthier.

*Here are all the short & simple SOS*
*(Stop Only Sugar) Diet Rules!*

**Rule 1** – Low Sugar
**Rule 2** – High Fiber
**Rule 3** – No More Rules!

(Of course, everybody's favorite "rule" is rule number 3!)

# 15. Colon Cleansing
# Very Bad Advice and Potentially Dangerous
# Just Don't Do It!

Let me offer you my professional opinion regarding the so-called "colon cleansing". First, your body is not capable of accumulating any toxins or waste in the wall of the colon. The colon cleansing claim is that you must remove all the evil toxins and waste collected in the wall of your colon, and then you will magically lose about 5 to 25 pounds almost instantly. Sorry folks, this does not and cannot happen. Your body and your digestive system just do not work this way.

Here are the most common claims made about colon cleansing. Colon cleansing will clean all the horrible and unhealthy toxins and waste that have accumulated in the wall of the colon over the years. After colon cleansing, one will be slim and trim, will magically lose any "beer belly", any "love handles" will fall off, and the colon, and therefore the person, will become much more healthy. All of these claims are absurd and completely false.

Colon cleansing actually represents perhaps the most "un-natural" thing you could ever do to your colon. Your colon functions as the "waste disposal system" of your body. The only natural state of the colon is to have stool and bacteria throughout the colon and rectum, and it gets very, very unhappy when it is too clean!

Now, how can I make such an outrageous claim that disputes all the colon cleansing benefits that are advertised using all their convincing statements about the accumulation of this dangerous waste in your colon? Well, the evidence is very simple, very logical, and very convincing. Be aware of two major points of scientific evidence; (1) every week, you get a brand new lining in your colon (mucosa), and (2) if you do not have stool and bacteria in your colon, you develop an inflammation in your colon, which is called diversion or disuse colitis (colon inflammation), with resulting severe diarrhea and rectal bleeding.

Here is a very important scientific fact about the lining of your colon, called the mucosa. Since it is so busy being your waste disposal department, the lining of your colon is one of the most active parts of your body. Let me repeat myself, the inner lining or your colon replaces itself about once a week by shedding cells and growing new ones. This lining (mucosa) is the part of the colon that actively absorbs water and electrolytes (mostly sodium and potassium) as the "waste" material passes through the colon. The absorption of water and electrolytes is a very important function of your colon to prevent dehydration and maintain normal electrolyte levels in your bloodstream.

Know that your colon will stay very healthy without pouring in all those laxatives and/or doing any of the so-called "colon cleansing". Further, a too clean colon will only get you and your colon in trouble, and this may wind up being a potentially serious digestive system trouble! Always remember that we all get a new colon lining each and every week.

Here's the bottom line regarding colon cleansing. There is no way your colon is capable of accumulating any toxins or excess waste in its wall. Colon cleansing is very un-natural and potentially dangerous. Again, your colon is designed to have stool and bacteria passing through it and it gets very, very unhappy when it is too clean.

# 16. Anal Itching (Pruritus Ani)
## "Help me, my butt is very itchy."

I often see patients with a complaint of anal irritation and itching. Anal itching is very bothersome and is usually the reason the person decides to seek medical help. Generally, the patient has already tried many of the over-the-counter anal creams, ointments, and suppositories and they often get no relief from the anal itching. The official medical wording for the diagnosis of anal itching is "Pruritus Ani". This medical diagnosis is very properly named, because "Pruritus Ani" is the Latin term for "Itchy Anus". The medical term "perianal" describes the location as being "around the anal opening".

Anal itching may be off and on, or may be present every day. In severe cases, there is an intense anal itching all day long and the itching may be severe enough to even keep a person awake at night. Without proper treatment, the perianal tissues may become inflamed and irritated to the point of causing slight rectal bleeding with bowel movements, and blood spotting may also be seen on the tissue after wiping. Of course, all rectal bleeding must be evaluated by your health care provider to be certain the true source of the bleeding is identified.

Certainly, it is appropriate to gently cleanse the anal area when bathing, but not to excess. With anal itching, patients often believe this is caused from the anal area not being clean enough. Therefore, patients with anal itching and irritation frequently and aggressively wash their anal area when they shower or take a bath. They may also wash this area after each bowel movement.

Here is what people with anal itching really need to know. **Excess cleansing of the perianal area is the CAUSE of the anal itching and irritation!**

Here is what happens with overzealous and excess perianal cleansing. When the perianal skin initially becomes irritated and inflamed, the body naturally lays down epithelial (skin) cells to heal the perianal area as part of the body's normal healing process. If the itching persists, it is logical to believe that the anal area must not be clean enough. So, we then come along with our bar of soap, wash cloth, and frequently scrub this area vigorously. Well, guess what! We just washed off all the cells trying to heal this area, and the inflammation, irritation, and itching only gets worse! Further, because of the strong anti-bacterial properties of most bars of soap, a perianal yeast infection will often develop, and this adds significantly to the itching.

The following is a very effective way to get rid of the anal itching and irritation. First, one MUST stop all soap and excess cleansing of the anal area. When irritated, the anal area should only be cleaned with water, and generally no more than once a day. There should be no scrubbing of the anal area. Following a shower, the area should be gently patted dry. I recommend an over-the-counter anti-yeast cream such as Lotrimin (clotrimazole) cream, or generic brand, with only a small amount to be applied to the anal area twice a day for 7 to 10 days. A high fiber diet with daily fiber supplements will prevent diarrhea and/or constipation, both of which can irritate the anal canal. If you have persistent anal irritation, be sure to see your health care provider to properly diagnose the cause. It will most likely be from the most common cause of anal itching – excess perianal cleansing!

# 17. Anal Fissures
# Anal Pain During and After Bowel Movements

First, let us review the medical definition of an anal fissure. An anal fissure is a small sore spot located about one half inch inside the anal opening. The symptoms of an anal fissure are pain and/or bleeding during and after bowel movements. The pain can be severe and there may also be a small amount of rectal bleeding from the anal fissure during bowel movements. Anal fissures may also be called anal ulcers.

The most common cause of an anal fissure is the passage of a large, hard stool which tears the lining of the anal canal just inside the anal opening. Of course, this will most commonly occur when a person is constipated and they may not have had a recent normal bowel movement. Severe frequent diarrhea may also cause an anal fissure, but diarrhea is a much less common cause of an anal fissure.

Let us now review the recommended treatment for anal fissures. I always recommend a high fiber diet with fiber supplements, such as Sugar-free Metamucil and always advise my patients to be sure to take their fiber supplement every day, to keep their stools soft and easy to pass. If the anal fissure pain is severe, and it can be, I may also recommend and prescribe anesthetic anal creams or ointments. If there is no improvement on the high fiber diet, or if the anal fissure has been present for a longer period of time, minor outpatient surgical procedure for the anal fissure will likely be recommended.

Here is a brief summary of the surgical procedure done to treat an anal fissure. The human anal canal has two muscles, called the internal and external anal sphincter muscles. These muscles are used to close the anal canal to prevent the leakage of stool and gas out of the rectum. Sometimes, the internal sphincter muscle does not relax properly during a bowel movement and the anal canal does not open properly. Therefore, the passage of stool may then cause a small tear in the anal canal. This tear, known as an anal fissure, is painful during and after bowel movements. Anal fissure surgery involves making a small partial cut into this internal sphincter muscle to allow it to properly relax during a bowel movement. After this relatively minor out-patient surgery, the vast majority of anal fissures will heal within a few weeks. This is generally a very highly successful anal surgery. Patients are nearly always very satisfied with the results as they have no more pain during and after bowel movements.

Anal fissures do not lead to more serious problems like cancer. However, it is very important to note that all rectal bleeding should be evaluated by a qualified health care provider. Rectal bleeding may represent a more serious condition such as colon or rectal polyps or cancer, and the source of all rectal bleeding must always be accurately determined. We may also recommend further studies to assess the rectal bleeding, even if a person has a known anal fissure. It is always extremely important to discuss any rectal bleeding symptoms with your health care provider.

# 18. Hemorrhoids
## We Are All Born With Them,
## and Here is How to Take Care of Them!

Hemorrhoids are a normal part of the human anatomy and we all have them. Fortunately, most people do not have any problems with their hemorrhoids and therefore, are not even aware of their presence. Hemorrhoids are medically defined as the small arteries and veins in and around the anal canal. They provide the blood supply to the tissues of the anus and the anal sphincter muscles that we use for control of our intestinal gas and bowel movements. We all have three internal hemorrhoid blood vessels and three small external hemorrhoid blood vessels for a total of six places where these hemorrhoid blood vessels are located. Anatomically, one of these hemorrhoid blood vessel locations is always on the left side and two are always located on the right side.

The three internal hemorrhoids are located about one inch up inside the anal canal where it is attached to the lower rectum. The three external hemorrhoids are located on the outside of the where the anus meets the skin around our anal canal. Again, we have two places where the hemorrhoids are on the right side, named the right anterior hemorrhoids and the right posterior hemorrhoids, and one place where the hemorrhoids are on the left side, named the left lateral hemorrhoids.

Let us now review the potential problems we may have with our hemorrhoids. Any medical problems we may have with our internal hemorrhoids or with our external hemorrhoids are very different. Know that there are no pain sensing nerves attached to our internal hemorrhoids, so we never feel any pain from these internal hemorrhoids. There many pain sensing nerves attached to our external hemorrhoids, and our external hemorrhoids will always left us know if they are not happy! Let us next review any potential health problems we may have with either our internal hemorrhoids or with our external hemorrhoids.

The most common medical problem we may have with our internal hemorrhoids is painless bright red rectal bleeding. There may be no apparent cause, or this bleeding may be caused by constipation from hard stools or from diarrhea from passing very frequent stools, Bleeding from our internal hemorrhoids may also be caused by blood thinning medications such as aspirin or NSAIDs (Non-steroidal Anti-inflammatory Drugs such as ibuprofen, and others) or may also be caused from being on prescription blood-thinning medications. Of course, any and all rectal bleeding must be promptly evaluated to determine the exact source of the bleeding.

The most common medical problem we see from our external hemorrhoids is swelling near the anal opening with moderate to severe pain from a blood clot forming in the external hemorrhoid. This blood clot nearly always comes from a leaking vein, leading to the formation of a usually very painful swollen blood clot very near the anal opening. This is called a thrombosed (clotted) external hemorrhoid, and anyone who has ever had one knows that these can be very painful. Many of these will resolve on their own, by passing the blood clot out of the swollen hemorrhoid, or the clot may be reabsorbed back into our blood stream. If the pain is too severe, then the swollen area of the thrombosed external hemorrhoid should be treated with a small incision, and the blood clot will then be easily removed, with almost instant pain relief.

One of the best ways to prevent any internal and external hemorrhoid problems is to follow a high fiber diet, with 25 to 30 grams of fiber every day, perhaps with daily fiber supplements, and be sure to stay well hydrated with water and other low sugar fluids. If a person has no fluid restrictions, we should all take in a minimum of 60 ounces of fluid every day. It can be water, coffee, tea, or other low-sugar juices or sugar-free electrolyte drinks. Remember my 60/60 rule – our human body is 60 percent water and we all need at least 60 ounces of fluid each and every day! And yes, these are Doctor's Orders!

## About Your Author
## James A. Surrell, M.D.
Fellow, American College of Surgeons (ACS)

Fellow, American Society of Colon and Rectal Surgeons (ASCRS)

Dr. Surrell is a board-certified colorectal surgeon who holds fellowship status in both the American Society of Colon and Rectal Surgeons and the American College of Surgeons. He devoted 14 years to formal education with 4 years of pre-med at Northern Michigan University, 4 years of medical school at Michigan State University, 5 years of general surgery residency and one year of colorectal surgery fellowship. He has been a practicing colorectal surgeon for the past 20 plus years. In addition to the best-selling *SOS (Stop Only Sugar) Diet* book, Dr. Surrell has authored many articles in various medical journals on topics related to his specialty of colorectal surgery and digestive health. He is also the author of the personal motivation book, *The ABC's For Success in All We Do.*

Dr. Jim, or "Doc" (as he prefers to be called) is also a much sought-after speaker and speaks frequently to local, regional, and national public and professional groups. He blends a significant amount of humor into his many talks and is generally available to speak to nearly any group with an interest in learning more about various topics, including: our personal digestive health, diet and weight loss, cholesterol reduction, healthy nutrition, cancer prevention, and other healthy lifestyle topics. He also appears frequently on various TV programs, and writes a very popular Marquette Mining Journal newspaper column entitled: "Talk with the Doc".

Here is Dr. Jim Surrell's favorite quote:

"There isn't much humor in medicine, but there is a lot of medicine in humor."

# Other Books By Dr. James Surrell

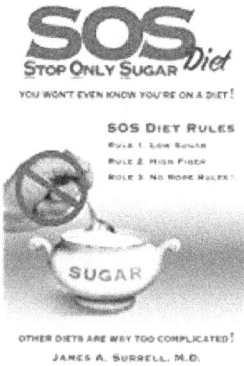

Other diets are way too complicated! The SOS (Stop Only Sugar) Diet has only three simple rules: Rule 1. Low Sugar, Rule 2. High Fiber, and everybody's favorite is Rule 3. No More Rules! The short and simple SOS Diet, by Digestive Health expert James A. Surrell, MD, involves only a minor lifestyle change. You too will soon become a "Label Reading Detective" and easily and almost effortlessly lose 5 to 8 pounds per month. Like so many others who have never lost weight on any other program, you too will be very successful on the SOS Diet. Get started today!  6 x 9 - 144 pages - $19.95

This short and simple ABC book will give you a review of time-tested and proven basic concepts that will guide you along your path to personal success. As you bring these ABC's into your way of thinking, this will serve as your guide to make good choices. Our important personal choices include what we choose to think about, our choice of spoken and written words, and how we choose to interact with others.  So get started today as you choose to have a positive attitude, choose to believe in yourself, and you will indeed be on your way to personal success. 5.5 x 8.5 - 64 pages - $14.95

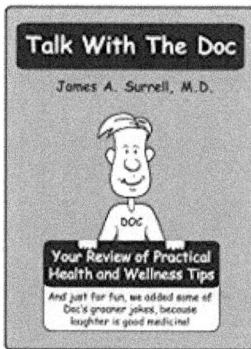

Dr. Jim Surrell writes newspaper columns entitled: "Talk With the Doc". This book represents a compilation of many of his very popular newspaper columns. He goes to great lengths to his make his columns brief, straight-forward, and easy to understand. In this regard, he avoids "doctor talk" with his writing as well as when he speaks to his patients and various public groups. His newspaper columns briefly review a large variety of various medical issues and items of interest with the intent of helping people improve their personal health and wellness. Many of the subjects in the columns contained in this book review topics that have been requested by his many readers  8.5 x 11 - 72 pages - $12.95

Books are Available at

Local Book Stores and
Globe Printing, Ishpeming MI

and at Amazon.com
in paperback or as a kindle instant download

www.ingramcontent.com/pod-product-compliance
Lightning Source LLC
Chambersburg PA
CBHW071643050426
42443CB00026B/954